Big Buck
Gives, Saves, and Spends

Written by Mark Goldman
Illustrated by Koen Setyawan

Buck loved helping Nana wash dishes and clean up.

Nana liked Buck helping her. She gave Buck ten dimes. He wondered what he could do with them.

The next day Buck decided he wanted a toy, so Mama took him to the store. He bought a toy for eight dimes.

At home, Buck wondered what to do with his last dime. The piggy bank would be a good place to keep it! Mama and Papa were so proud of Buck.

Buck got bigger and kept helping with chores around the house. He was a good helper. Mama and Papa gave him a dollar every week.

Big Buck got to go buy a toy with his money once a month.

Buck was running out of room in his piggy bank, so he needed a bigger piggy! Mama and Papa helped him find a better place for his savings.

Now Buck has his own daughter. He is a Papa!

Check out Big Buck's sister book!

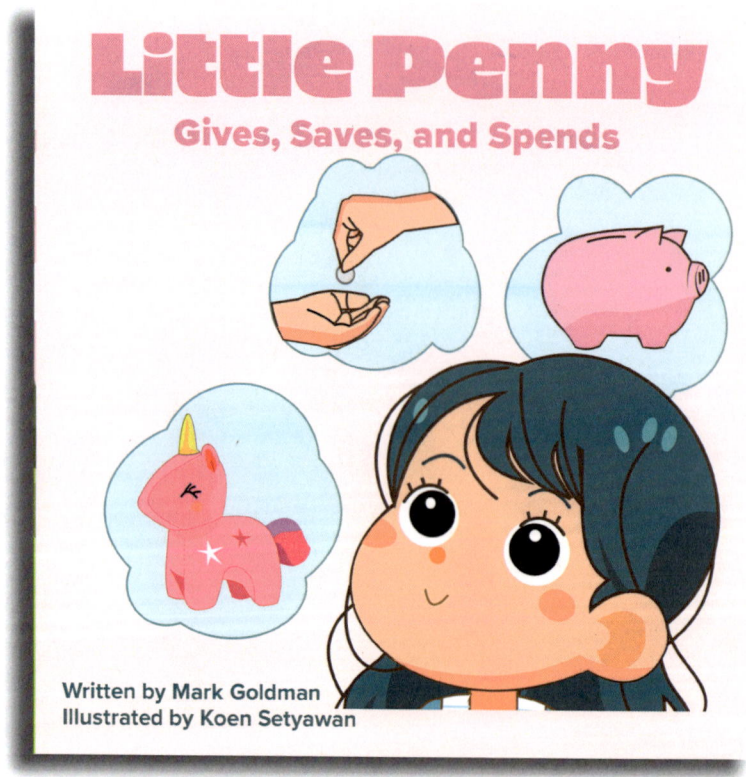

Note From the Author

I wrote this book because I was fortunate to have loving parents that taught me the importance of both giving and saving. As far as the spending was concerned, that came naturally.

My hope for the child you are reading this book to is that they will also learn the value of both giving and saving early in life, and that they will develop beneficial habits that stick with them for a lifetime.

May God bless you greatly for reading to this child.

-Mark Goldman

www.give-save-spend.com

published by
Fox Tales Children's Books

A division of Our Written Lives, LLC
San Antonio, Texas
www.OurWrittenLives.com

Mark Goldman ©2024
Art by Koen Setyawan

ISBN: 978-1-942923-88-6 (Hardback)

Fonts licensed for commercial use.

www.ingramcontent.com/pod-product-compliance
Lightning Source LLC
Chambersburg PA
CBRC092116280426
43673CB00082B/419